AF702336

Jan Becker

Making Money with statistical Arbitrage

Generating Alpha in sideway Markets with this Option Strategy

Anchor Compact

Becker, Jan: Making Money with statistical Arbitrage: Generating Alpha in sideway Markets with this Option Strategy. Hamburg, Diplomica Verlag GmbH 2012
Original title of the thesis: Hedge Funds Strategies – Time Series Based Semi-Variance Prediction Model For Statistical Arbitrage

ISBN: 978-3-95489-013-2
Print: Anchor Academic Publishing, an Imprint of Diplomica® Verlag GmbH, Hamburg, 2012
Additionally: Diplomica Verlag GmbH, Hamburg, Deutschland, Fachbuch,

Bibliographical Information of the German National Library:
The German National Library lists this publication in the German National Bibliography. Detailed bibliographic data can be found at: http://dnb.d-nb.de

The digital publication (eBook) of this work with the ISBN 978-3-95489-513-7 can be purchased on the general market or directly from the publisher.

All rights reserved. This publication may not be reproduced, stored in a retrieval system or transmitted, in any form or by any means, electronic, mechanical, photocopying, recording or otherwise, without the prior permission of the publishers.

Dieses Werk ist urheberrechtlich geschützt. Die dadurch begründeten Rechte, insbesondere die der Übersetzung, des Nachdrucks, des Vortrags, der Entnahme von Abbildungen und Tabellen, der Funksendung, der Mikroverfilmung oder der Vervielfältigung auf anderen Wegen und der Speicherung in Datenverarbeitungsanlagen, bleiben, auch bei nur auszugsweiser Verwertung, vorbehalten. Eine Vervielfältigung dieses Werkes oder von Teilen dieses Werkes ist auch im Einzelfall nur in den Grenzen der gesetzlichen Bestimmungen des Urheberrechtsgesetzes der Bundesrepublik Deutschland in der jeweils geltenden Fassung zulässig. Sie ist grundsätzlich vergütungspflichtig. Zuwiderhandlungen unterliegen den Strafbestimmungen des Urheberrechtes.

Die Wiedergabe von Gebrauchsnamen, Handelsnamen, Warenbezeichnungen usw. in diesem Werk berechtigt auch ohne besondere Kennzeichnung nicht zu der Annahme, dass solche Namen im Sinne der Warenzeichen- und Markenschutz-Gesetzgebung als frei zu betrachten wären und daher von jedermann benutzt werden dürften.

Die Informationen in diesem Werk wurden mit Sorgfalt erarbeitet. Dennoch können Fehler nicht vollständig ausgeschlossen werden, und die Diplomarbeiten Agentur, die Autoren oder Übersetzer übernehmen keine juristische Verantwortung oder irgendeine Haftung für evtl. verbliebene fehlerhafte Angaben und deren Folgen.

© Anchor Academic Publishing, ein Imprint der Diplomica® Verlag GmbH
http://www.diplom.de, Hamburg 2012
Printed in Germany

1.1 Abstract

In the following study I am going to present a short survey of the hedge fund industry, its regulation and the existent hedge fund strategies. Especially statistical arbitrage is explained in further detail and major performance measurement ratios are presented. In the second part, I am going to introduce a semi-variance model for statistical arbitrage. The model is compared to the standard Garch model, which is so often used in daily option trading, derivate pricing and risk management. Because investment returns are not equally distributed over time, sources for statistical arbitrage occur. The semi-variance model takes skewness into account and provides higher returns at lower volatility than the Garch model. The concept is aimed to be a synopsis of mean reversion and chart pattern detection. The computer model is generated with respect to Brownian motion and technical analysis and provides significant returns to the investment. As market efficiency hypothesis states the impossibility of arbitrage opportunities over the long run, on the other hand market anomalies significantly outstand. Connecting both elements creates a profitable trading system. The combination of both approaches delivers a sensible hedge fund concept. The out-of-sample backtest verifies out-performance and implies the need for further research in the area of higher moment CAPM and additional market timing strategies as sources of statistical arbitrage.

1.2 Structure

After giving a short survey of the hedge fund industry and the existent hedge fund strategies, statistical arbitrage is explained in further detail. In the second part a semi-variance model is compared to the Garch model. Its prediction power is stress tested and a backtest on the DAX30-Index performed. Therefore Value at Risk, Expected Shortfall and many other risk measurement ratios are taken into consideration. The appendix presents further ideas for research and possible expansions of the model.

1.3 Table of Contents

Part I	1.1 Abstract	p. I
	1.2 Structure	p. I
	1.3 Table of Contents	p. II
	1.4 List of Abbreviations	p. III
	1.5 List of Figures and Tables	p. IV
Part II	2.1 Overview of the Hedge Fund Industry	p. 1
Part III	3.1 Hedge Fund Strategies Overview	p. 3
	3.2 Statistical Arbitrage in Detail	p. 8
	3.3 Performance Analysis	p. 10
Part IV	4.1 State of the Art in Research	p. 16
	4.2 Principles of Garch	p. 20
	4.3 Introduction of a Semi -Variance Model	p. 22
	4.3.1 Methodology	p. 22
	4.3.2 Description of Market Data	p. 23
	4.3.3 Prediction Power	p. 26
	4.3.4 Risk Measurement	p. 27
	4.4 Backtest with Real Options	p. 28
	4.4.1 Out-of-Sample Market Data	p. 29
	4.4.2 Performance Comparison	p. 30
Part V	5.1 Conclusion	p. 31
	5.2 Further Research	p. 32
Part VI	6.1 List of Literature	p. 34
	6.2 Appendix	p. 41

1.4 List of Abbreviations

BR	Burke-ratio
CR	Calmar-ratio
CSFB	Credit Swiss First Boston
CSR	Conditional Sharpe-ratio
DAX	Deutscher Aktien Index
EFAMA	European Fund and Asset Management Association
ERVaR	Excess return on Value at Risk
Euwax	European Warrant Exchange
Garch	Generalized autoregressive conditional heteroskedasticity
HFR	Hedge Fund Research
HPM	Higher-partial-moment
K3	Kappa 3
LPM	Lower-partial-moments
MSR	Modified Sharpe-ratio
SOR	Sortino-Ratio
SR	Sharpe-ratio
STR	Sterling-ratio
VaR	Value at Risk
UPR	Upper-potential-ratio

Mathematical variables of formulas are defined directly in the text.

1.5 List of Figures and Tables

Figure 1:	Hedge fund strategies overview
Figure 2:	Average hedge fund strategy returns as of 2009 (Absolute-report (2010))
Figure 3:	Chart pattern conversion to binary code
Figure 4:	DAX-Chart from 1990-2010
Figure 5:	JB-test on 30 days DAX returns
Figure 6:	Negative and positive skew
Figure 7:	Historical DAX upper and lower semi-variance
Figure 8:	Model Accuracy on DAX
Figure 9:	Garch and semi-variance-model in comparison.
Figure 10:	Option spread strategy
Figure 11:	Payoff-diagram of options spread strategy
Figure 12:	Hedge fund annualized return comparison (CSFB (2209))
Figure 13:	Hedge fund index performance (Absolute-report (2010))
Figure 14:	Worldwide investment fund assets by (EFAMA (2010))
Figure 15:	Composition of worldwide investment fund asset (EFAMA (2010))

Table 1:	Monthly performance (*CSFB* (2010))
Table 2:	Value at Risk (5%, 20day) for DAX, Garch and Semi-variance-model
Table 3:	Shortfall of DAX, Garch and Semi-variance-model
Table 4:	Overview of performance measures on backtest
Table 5:	Options traded for the backtest
Table 6:	Largest hedge funds (Market Folly(2010))

PART II

2.1 Overview of the Hedge Fund Industry

The hedge fund industry has grown from as few as 300 funds in 1990 to more than a $2 trillion industry with 10,000 active funds today. *EFAMA* (2009) stated that investment fund assets worldwide reached EUR 15.9 trillion at the end of 2009. The very first hedge fund was started by Alfred W. Jones in 1949. By using leverage and short selling, he effectively "hedged" risk in the marketplace. Hedge funds can take both long and short positions, make concentrated investments, use leverage or derivatives, and invest in many markets. This is in sharp contrast to mutual funds, which are highly regulated and cannot easily take advantage the same breadth of investment instruments. Many hedge fund strategies seek to reduce market risk specifically by shorting equities or derivatives. There are a multitude of different strategies used by hedge fund managers today, and the term "hedge" doesn't always apply, since many of these funds are not hedged at all. In fact, many hedge funds take positions that are often highly speculative. Hedge funds are thought to provide returns that are uncorrelated with traditional investments. Their returns over a sustained period of time have outperformed standard equity and bond indexes with less volatility and less risk of loss than equities. Investing in hedge funds tends to be favoured by more sophisticated investors, who understand the private consequences of major stock market corrections. Many endowments and pension funds allocate assets to hedge funds. Most hedge funds are highly specialized, relying on the specific expertise of the manager or management team. Hedge funds are primarily organized as private partnerships to provide maximum flexibility in constructing a portfolio. Most hedge fund managers commit a portion of their wealth to the funds further aligning their interest with that of other investors. Many hedge fund strategies, particularly arbitrage strategies, are limited as to how much capital they can successfully employ before returns diminish. As a result, many successful hedge fund managers limit the amount of capital they will accept. It is important to understand the differences between the various hedge fund strategies. Investment returns, volatility, and risk vary among the different hedge fund strategies. Some strategies are able to deliver consistent returns with extremely low risk of loss, while others may be as or more volatile than mutual funds. The main purpose of hedge funds is to achieve positive returns independently of capital market movements.

Hedge Fund Risks

Investing in hedge funds implies several forms of risk. The appetite for risk can involve large losses (For example by strategies involving out the money option writing, leverage, short selling or high yield bonds, distressed securities and collateralized debt obligations based on sub-prime mortgages). Not only the known factors of operational and market risks have to be taken into account, but also the risks of transparency and regulation. Additionally to fewer jurisdictions from regulators, there are also less public disclosure requirements.

Fees

a) The manager's performance fee is calculated as a percentage of the fund's profits, usually counting both realized and unrealized profits. Performance fees align the interests of manager and investor more closely than flat fees do. Typically, hedge funds charge 20% of returns as a performance fee.

b) A high water mark means that the manager receives performance fees only on increases in the net asset value of the fund in excess of the highest net asset value it has previously achieved.

c) Some managers specify a hurdle rate, signifying that they will not charge a performance fee until the fund's annualized performance exceeds a benchmark rate.

The legal structure of a specific hedge fund – in particular its domicile and the type of legal entity used – is usually determined by the tax environment of the fund's expected investors. Regulatory considerations will also play a role. Many hedge funds are established in offshore financial centres so that the fund can avoid paying tax on the increase in the value of its portfolio. An investor will still pay tax on any profit it makes when it realizes its investment, and the investment manager, usually based in a major financial centre, will pay tax on the fees that it receives for managing the fund.

Around 60% of hedge funds were registered in offshore locations in 2009. The Cayman Islands was the most popular registration location and accounted for 39% of the number of global hedge funds. It was followed by Delaware (US) 27%, British Virgin Islands 7% and Bermuda 5%. Around 5% of global hedge funds are registered in the EU, primarily in Ireland and Luxembourg

To verify a non-fraud, offshore management companies often provide the latest audited annual and semi-annual report without being obliged to. Moreover the contractual terms and conditions and sales prospectuses or equivalent documents, information on organization, management, investment policy, risk management and custodian bank or a comparable institution and information on investment restrictions, liquidity, the extent of the leverage and the carrying out of short sales are published.

PART III

3.1 Hedge Fund Strategies Overview

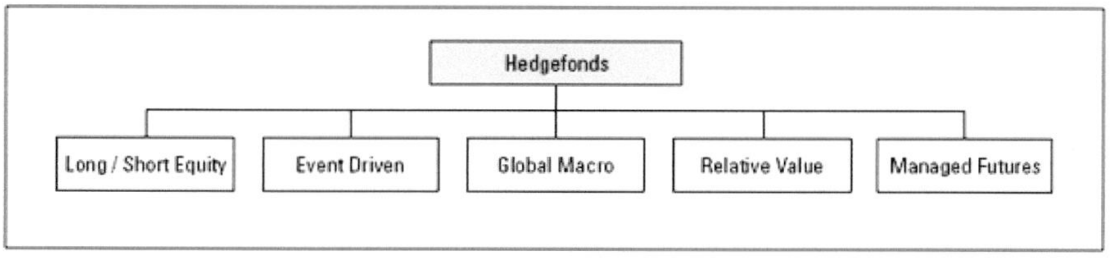

Figure 1

In current practice, hedge funds strategies are classified following *CSFB* (2010) and *HFR* (20110). For classification in literature please read the papers by *Injic and Heen* (2003) or *Agarwal and Naik* (2000). The following overview is based on Dieter Kaiser (2003).The distinction between the different hedge fund strategies is often based on the following criteria: style, markets, instruments, exposure, sectors, method and diversification.

3.1.1 Long/Short Equity – make money on alpha

Overview

Long/short equity hedge fund managers buy undervalued stocks and sell the overvalued. Stock-picking is the key to outperformance in this discipline. Long-term holding, patience, and strong discipline are often required until the ultimate intrinsic value or potential worth is recognized by the market. Many managers use pair trades, where one stock is sold against another. Both stocks are of the same sector. If there are more stocks bought than sold, it is called a long bias. Vice versa a net short position is called a short bias. Typically a long bias implies directional trading in sense of a bull market.

Equity Hedge

The paradigm of equity hedge is absolute return achieved independently from the actual market movement. The fund can be market neutral or net long or net short - conditionally on the market situation. The manager combines leverage, short positions and stock picking. Partly derivatives are used.

Equity-Non-Hedge

Mutual funds concentrate on stock picking and research, whereas equity-non-hedge also has the freedom to apply leverage. This is the only distinction.

Short Selling

Short selling strategies sell securities without coverage. Thereby anticipating to rebuy them at a future date at a lower price. The manager assesses the securities to be overvalued.

3.1.2 Relative Value – Make Money on Spreads

Overview

Anomalies in the prices of identical underlyings at different exchanges are exploited. The riskless profit is called an arbitrage. Market risk should be decreased to zero. Market neutrality is not to be mistaken for "risk less". Sometimes leverage up to 100 times of equity value is used in order to sufficiently generate profits on spreads.

Fixed Income Arbitrage

Bonds and other fixed income derivatives are traded in fixed income arbitrage. The strategy is based on historical correlation of yields followed by a change. Fund managers supposed the spread to mean revert to historical levels and take a profit. Often similar underlyings are traded like government bonds versus non government bonds with AAA rating

Credit Spread Arbitrage

Credit risks are valuated by the fund manager and the underlying securities are bought long or short. The strategy is similar to equity long/short, but dependant on the evaluation of the issuer's credit rating. It can be via derivatives, asset backed securities, collateralized debt obligations or the underlying itself.

Capital-Structure-Arbitrage

This form of arbitrage profits from excess demand and psychological factors. Those are reflected in the short term imbalance of price between junior and senior debt.

Yield Curve Arbitrage

Given the actual yield curve, government bonds and its difference to corporate bonds, this hedge fund strategy gains value by yield curve changes.

Mortgage-Backed Securities

Hedge fund managers buy mortgage-back securities with the right of early repayment thus the risk premium is higher. The manager has to control two risks. If interest rate decreases, the house owner will refinances with lower interest rate and the security is paid out. On the other hand, if interest rate rises too far, the security will be reduced in price due to the initiation of higher yield instruments. To cover for duration exposure similar securities or derivatives are sold.

Convertible Bond Arbitrage

This strategy seeks to profit from the pricing of the embedded option in a convertible bond. Often used is a long convertible position with a corresponding short position in the underlying stock. Varying degrees of leverage are employed with this strategy. The combination results in a positive net cash flow whether the stock price increases or decreases.

Stock-Index-Arbitrage

A stock basket is traded against its representative index. Relative value discrepancies are skimmed with options or futures. Long or short positions in both directions are common.

Split Strike Conversions

Additionally to the underlying, a call with higher strike is sold, whereas a put with lower strike is bought. In both market phases the position will be profitable. In a down market the call premium delivers value, while the put hedges the underlying. In an up market the performance is limited to the call strike minus put premium. Only in a side market the paid put option premium is not offset by stock return. This strategy can also be inversed.

Statistical Arbitrage

Statistical arbitrage usually engages in very short term trading and residual mean reversion. Statistical computer models trade on quantitative models with high frequency. The portfolio often is market neutral.

3.1.3 Event Driven – make money on events

Overview

This strategy aims to profit from price imbalances resulting from a specific event or transaction in a life cycle of a business - for example, merger, hostile takeover, or leveraged buyout.

Merger Arbitrage

This strategy involves taking position in companies that are either currently or likely to be engaged in corporate mergers and acquisitions. Shares of the target are purchased, whereas stocks of the acquirer are sold. Risks are regulatory, financial, company-specific or antitrust reasons. The profit is made on the narrowing spread.

Distressed Securities

This strategy invests in illiquid debt and/or equity of firms in or near bankruptcy in order to profit from a potential recovery. As well as long positions in the stock, short positions in the debt are applied. These profits are generated from the market's lack of understanding of the true value of the deeply discounted securities. Results generally are not dependent on the direction of the markets.

High Yield

Low rated bonds with no historical earnings or complete revenue track record, but high yield is part of the portfolio in this strategy. The implied risk is offset by put options on the bond or call options on stocks which would profit on the default of the underlying.

Special Situations

This strategy invests in event-driven situations such as mergers, hostile takeovers, reorganizations or leveraged buy outs. It may involve simultaneous purchase of stock in companies being acquired and the sale of stock in its acquirer, hoping to profit from the spread between the current market price and the ultimate purchase price of the company. The manager may also utilize derivatives to leverage returns and to hedge out interest rate or market risk. Results are generally not dependent on direction of market.

Regulation D

Private equity transactions can be found in this section. In exchange for equity a convertible is issued which is not exchange traded. The warrant has no fixed strike price. The hedge fund manager sells additionally to the long convertible position a stock and an option. At maturity the conversion is discussed with the company. Until maturity a sale of the convertible is not possible on exchange, because there is no liquid market.

3.1.4 Global Macro – make money on trends

Overview

An opportunistic, "top-down" approach is implemented by managers using this macroeconomic strategy. Trades are based upon major changes in the global economy, including interest rates and currencies, as well as changes in the economic policies of specific countries. Macro strategies use leverage. Relative valuation of financial instruments is within the strategy as well as market dynamics and sentiment. The manager tries to exploit perceived divergences between and within various asset classes. Returns are made by a correct forecast of global market performances.

Currencies

The fund manager encumbers with debt in a currency he sees overvalued and invests in a currency which is relatively undervalued. While the manager focuses on relative value trends, three-point-arbitrage is mentioned here as a spread strategy. In three-point-arbitrage currency is changed back over two other currencies (for example USD/EUR to EUR/CHF to CHF/USD).

Emerging Markets

Investments in equity or debt of emerging markets which tend to have higher inflation and volatile growth. Some emerging market countries are Brazil, China, India, and Russia. The major emerging market areas are Latin America, Eastern Europe, Asia, and the Pacific Rim. Various asset classes with different strategies are used. Short selling is not permitted in many emerging markets and therefore effective hedging is often not available and buy-and-hold-strategies are most common.

Market Timing

Market timing strategies switch among various asset classes to time price movements in different markets. Stocks, bonds, mutual funds, and money market funds are some of the asset classes used. Assets among different asset classes are allocated depending on the manager's view of the economic or market outlook. Market movements and the timing entry and exit from markets are predicted by trend following strategies.

Commodities

A commodity strategy invests in material goods or its related futures. Examples are gold, oil, coffee or wheat. At the end of the holding period a profit can be generated by selling the underlying or the good. Arbitrage strategies can be applied hereby as well. Transition to the managed futures strategy is smooth.

3.2 Statistical Arbitrage in Detail

Origins of Statistical Arbitrage

Statistical arbitrage originated in the 1980s from the hedging demand created by Morgan Stanley's equity block trading desk operations. If the firm purchased a large block of shares, it would short a closely correlated stock to hedge against any major downturns in the market. Traders soon began to think of these pairs not as a block to be executed and its hedge, but rather two sides of a trading strategy aimed at profit making rather than simply hedging.

Statistical arbitrage refers to highly technical short-term mean-reversion strategies involving large numbers of securities, very short holding periods and substantial computational, trading, and IT infrastructure. It involves data mining and statistical methods, as well as automated trading systems. Statistical arbitrage is actually any strategy that is bottom-up, beta-neutral in approach and uses statistical or econometric techniques in order to provide signals for execution. Signals are often generated through a contrarian mean-reversion.

The goal is to construct a tradable stationary process so that trades are entered when the process reaches an extreme value, and exited when the process reverts to some mean value. Since market inefficiencies are generally small in magnitude, so transaction costs are one reason why inefficiencies remain.

Statistical arbitrage is subject to model weakness as well as stock-specific risk.

The statistical relationship on which the model is based may be spurious, or may break down due to changes in the distribution of returns on the underlying assets. Factors which the model may not be aware of having exposure to, could become the significant drivers of price action in the markets, and the inverse applies also. On a stock-specific level, there is risk of M&A activity or even default for an individual name. Such an event would immediately end any historical relationship assumed from empirical statistical analysis.

Statistical arbitrage has also caused some major problems, however. The most readily apparent was the Long Term Capital Management collapse, which almost left the market in ruins.

In the academic literature statistical arbitrage is opposed to deterministic arbitrage. In deterministic arbitrage a sure profit can be obtained from being long some securities and short others.

a) For arbitrage of typ 1, there is a sure payoff in the future, without the merit to pay anything today or even getting some money already now.

$$p'N \leq 0 \quad (1)$$

$$X*N > 0 \quad (2)$$

where p' is the price vector and N denotes the quantities of involved assets in a matrix. X is the payoff matrix.

b) Arbitrage of typ 2 delivers a payment today, but there is surely no payment in the future.

$$p'N < 0 \quad (3)$$

$$X*N \geq 0 \quad (4)$$

c) The combined contingent claim of both formulas must thus have a price of:

$$p^{(L+1)} = \sum_{l=0}^{L} N^{(l)} p^{(l)} \quad (5)$$

If this price is violated, an arbitrage opportunity is possible by the Law of One Price. The portfolio can be replicated and sold with profit.

In statistical arbitrage there is a statistical mispricing of one or more assets based on the expected value of these assets. Statistical arbitrage conjectures statistical mispricing or price relationships that are true in expectation, in the long run when repeating a trading strategy.

$$E(X*N) > 0 \tag{6}$$

Statistical arbitrage opportunity is a zero-cost trading strategy for which the conditional expected payoff in each final state of the economy is nonnegative. Unlike a pure arbitrage opportunity, a statistical arbitrage opportunity can have negative payoffs provided that the average payoff in each final state is non- negative (Bondarenko (2003)).

$$\sum_{i=0}^{\infty} E(X_i * N_i) \geq 0 \tag{7}$$

In the later analysis of statistical arbitrage option strategy the expected payoff will play a major role.

3.3 Performance Analysis

As many hedge fund manager aim to outperform the market, we have to find means how to compare the outcome of their results. As many strategies can provide very high returns, they often are also very volatile. The relation of profit and the amount of risk to achieve this result have to be in a reasonable proportion. The following chapter should help in getting a clearer view. Useful insights can be delivered by alpha, standard deviation, lower partial moments, drawdown and finally Value at Risk models.

Alpha

Measures the value that an investment manager produces, by comparing the manager's performance to that of a risk-free investment (usually a Treasury bill). Alpha can also be used as a measure of residual risk, relative to the market in which a fund participates.

$$\alpha_J = R_i - \lfloor R_f + \beta_{iM} * (R_M - R_f) \rfloor \tag{8}$$

where R_i is the portfolio's return, R_M the return of the market, R_f the risk-free rate and β_{iM} is the sensitivity of the expected asset returns to the expected market return. A fund manager thus only has positive alpha, if the funds performance is lager than the risk-free rate and moreover provides a risk adequate profit compared to the whole market as benchmark.

Performance Measures

A detailed overview of many performance measures is given by *Martin Eling* (2006).
There are many important ratios in literature. The maybe most important and most cited is the sharpe ratio by Modigliani(1997).

$$SR_i = \frac{r_i^d - r_f}{\sigma_i} \tag{9}$$

where r_i^d is the portfolio's return, r_f the risk- free rate which is sometimes also adjusted to a higher hurdle rate for more exact benchmarking and the standard deviation σ_i. This ratio compares the excess return to the volatility inhered.

Lower Partial Moments

Lower partial moments calculate the lower deviation from the given expected return. They are often measured by higher exponents to take investor's risk aversion into account.

$$LMP_{ni}(\tau) = \frac{1}{T}\sum_{1}^{T} \max[\tau - r_{it}, 0]^n \tag{10}$$

where τ is the average return and T is the number of regarded periods. First order partial moments can be interpreted as failure probability while lower partial moment of second can also be interpreted as the semi-variance.

Related performance measures are Omega Ω_i by *Shadwick and Keating* (2002), Sortino-Ratio SOR_i by *Sortino and van der Meer* (1991) and Kappa $K3_i$ by *Kaplan and Knowless* (2004). All three measures set relative outperformance in relation to the adjusted risk.

$$\Omega_i(\tau) = \frac{r_i^d - r_f}{LPM_{li}(\tau)} + 1 \tag{11}$$

$$SOR_i(\tau) = \frac{r_i^d - r_f}{\sqrt[2]{LPM_{2i}(\tau)}} \tag{12}$$

$$K3_i(\tau) = \frac{r_i^d - r_f}{\sqrt[3]{LPM_{3i}(\tau)}} \tag{13}$$

Upside-Potential-Ratio

Opposite to the average return is the upside-potential-ratio by *Sortino, van der Meer and Plantinga (*1999).

$$UPR_i(\tau) = \frac{\frac{1}{T}\sum_{1}^{T}\max[r_{it} - \tau, 0]^2}{\sqrt[2]{\frac{1}{T}\sum_{1}^{T}\max[\tau - r_{it}, 0]^2}} \tag{14}$$

Here upside movements are compared to downward movements relative to the average return or benchmark.

Drawdown

Young (1991), *Kestern* (1996) and *Burke* (1994) use a maximum drawdown method. This method is often used in commodity trading since spot prices do not fall down to zero. Goods tend to retain a minimum price as opposed to defaulted equities.

Young (1991) refers to the maximum drawdown MD_{i1} in his Calmar-ratio.

$$CR_i = \frac{r_i^d - r_f}{-MD_{i1}} \tag{15}$$

Whereas *Kestern* (1996) considers the mean drawdown to be a better performance indicator in his Sterling-ratio.

$$STR_i = \frac{r_i^d - r_f}{\frac{1}{D}\sum_{j=1}^{D} MD^2{}_i} \tag{16}$$

Burke (1994) expands this thought by adjusting the average drawdown to a ratio similar to the variance calculation procedure. Bigger drawdowns thus affect the ratio more than small drawdowns. The Burke-ratio is denoted as

$$BR_i = \frac{r_i^d - r_f}{\sqrt{\frac{1}{D}\sum_{j=1}^{D} MD_i^2}} \tag{17}$$

Value At Risk

Under Value at Risk the approximate loss with a specific probability is calculated under normal distribution assumption.

$$VaR_i = -(r_i^d + z_\alpha * \sigma_i) \tag{18}$$

where z_α is the assigned value in the standard normal distribution.

Adjusting the Value at Risk to CVaR, we get the maximum shortfall. This ratio explains the expected loss in the case of a significance level violation.

$$CVaR_i = E\left[-r_{it} \middle| r_{it} \leq -VaR_i\right] \tag{19}$$

The Value at Risk can also be modified by a Cornish-Fischer-method and adjusted to skew and kurtosis.

$$\begin{aligned} MVaR_i &= \\ -(r_i^d + \sigma_i &* (z_\alpha + (z_\alpha^2 - 1) * S_i / 6 + (z_\alpha^3 - 3 + z_\alpha) \\ + E_i / 24 &- (2 + z_\alpha^3 - 5 * z_\alpha) * S_i^2 / 36)) \end{aligned} \tag{20}$$

where S_i is the skew and E_i the excess of kurtosis. Both are defined as:

$$S_i = \frac{\frac{1}{T}\sum_{t=1}^{T}(r_{it} - r_i^d)^3}{\sigma_i^3} \tag{21}$$

$$E_i = \frac{\frac{1}{T}\sum_{t=1}^{T}(r_{it} - r_i^d)^4}{\sigma_i^4} - 3 \tag{22}$$

In application we get the Excess Return on Value at Risk by *Dowd* (2000)

$$ERVaR_i = \frac{r_i^d - r_f}{VaR_i} \tag{23}$$

The Conditional Sharpe ratio by *Artzner, Delbaen, Eber and Heath* (1999)

$$CSR_i = \frac{r_i^d - r_f}{CVaR_i} \qquad (24)$$

And the Modified Sharpe Ratio by *Gregoriou and Gueyie* (2003)

$$MSR_i = \frac{r_i^d - r_f}{MVaR_i} \qquad (25)$$

Please read *Martin Eling* (2006) for a complete analysis of all performance measurement ratios introduced above. The performance measurement ratios are necessary and will be applied later to the model.

Reality Check

Hedge funds returns have differed strongly in the year 2009. Convertible Arbitrage and long/short equity have been the most successful strategies in 2009. One of the weakest performers has been equity market neutral. The following figure displays the wide spread of returns between fund performance within one strategy.

2009 Average Strategy Returns (data as of December 31, 2009)

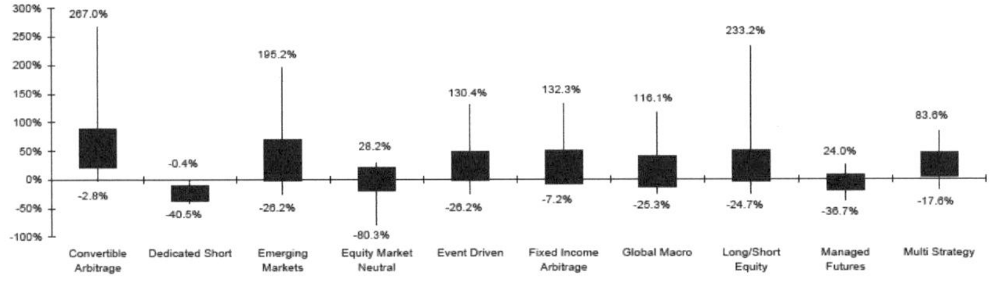

Figure 2

CSFB (2010) provides a survey of compared sharpe ratios. The global macro strategy showed the highest sharpe ratio of 0,85. Dedicated short bias has been the worst strategy with -0,34.

Monthly Performance (beginning Jan 1994) Mar 2010					
Index / Sub Strategies	Value	1 Year Return	Annl	Std Dev	Sharpe
Credit Suisse/Tremont Hedge Fund Index	429.14	21.20%	9.38%	7.76%	0.75
Convertible Arbitrage	338.08	41.62%	7.78%	7.17%	0.59
Dedicated Short Bias	60.44	-32.8%	-3.05%	16.91%	-0.39
Emerging Markets	352.95	33.51%	8.07%	15.46%	0.29
Equity Market Neutral	232.91	7.03%	5.34%	10.76%	0.17
Event Driven	498.81	26.36%	10.40%	6.04%	1.14
Distressed	574.39	28.48%	11.36%	6.66%	1.18
Multi-Strategy	465.39	24.99%	9.92%	6.41%	1.00
Risk Arbitrage	315.29	10.54%	7.32%	4.18%	0.91
Fixed Income Arbitrage	220.08	27.78%	4.97%	6.03%	0.24
Global Macro	666.71	11.55%	12.38%	10.23%	0.87
Long/Short Equity	493.63	22.41%	10.32%	10.00%	0.68
Managed Futures	271.08	-1.78%	6.33%	11.79%	0.24
Multi-Strategy	352.60	23.36%	8.19%	5.46%	0.85

Table 1

This short overview does not focus on describing all the differences in historical data and discussing the advantages and disadvantages regarding portfolio selection, but wants to introduce a semi-variance-model for statistical arbitrage.

PART IV

In the following section the recent concepts and opinions in literature are introduced and a short survey of market anomalies is provided. Then the Garch model is explained and many of the statistical arbitrage opportunities, which can be found in practice, are incorporated into a semi-variance model. The significant difference for this arbitrage opportunity are justified by papers on chart pattern prediction, time series analysis, momentum effects and the Garch model itself. In the concluding section a backtest with options on the DAX-Index verifies the outperformance of semi-variance model with skew.

4.1 State of the Art in Research

Market efficiency

The weak form of the market efficiency hypothesis implies that all information available in past prices must be reflected in the current price. This hypothesis implies that technical analysis is without merit in an efficient market. As investors compete to exploit their common knowledge of a stock's price history, they necessarily drive stock prices to levels where expected rate of return are exactly commensurate with risk. According to this hypothesis, technical analysis cannot predict future price behaviour. If the cost of transactions were considered, the returns could even be negative (Fama and Blume (1966), Jensen and Benington (1970)).

Chordia, Roll, and Subrahmanyam (2002) argue that information takes a minimum of time to be incorporated into price, in such a way that the market could be inefficient for a short time interval. Additionally in behavioural finance overconfidence, optimism and wishful thinking, representativeness, conservatism, and the belief perseverance are made responsible for price discrepancies which are not induced by fundamental risk, noise trader risk, short-sales constraints, cost of finding and learning about the mispricing and the cost of resources needed to exploit it. A strategy's implementation can often be both risky and costly, thereby allowing the mispricing to survive.

Random Walk

Adding this unknown factors to the equation, we can argue with *Malkiel Burton's* (1996) "random walk down wall street". In physics the effect of random movement is called a Brownian motion. In mathematical context it is a Wiener process:

$$\Delta z = \varepsilon\sqrt{\Delta t} \quad \text{with } \varepsilon \sim \mathrm{N}(0,1) \tag{26}$$

where z is a and t are variables and ε is a standard normal variable.

The formula for mean reversion to the true price can be denoted as an Ornstein–Uhlenbeck process

$$dx_t = \Theta(\mu - x_t)dt + \sigma dW_t \tag{27}$$

where $\theta > 0$, μ and $\sigma > 0$ are parameters and W_t denotes the Wiener process. Under Markov property, which means that the Wiener process given what has happened up to some time t, is the same as if the process had been started at the position X_t at time 0. An Itō diffusion has the important property of being *Markovian*

$$\Delta x = \alpha(x,t)\Delta t + \beta(x,t)\varepsilon\sqrt{\Delta t} \tag{28}$$

where α and β are parameters.

Previous studies on mean-reversion and contrarian strategies include *Lehmann* (1990), *Lo and MacKinlay* (1990) and *Poterba and Summers* (1988).

Application

Fama and French (1988) proposed a mean reverting model to explain stock price movements. They also found that autocorrelation of returns become strongly negative for a 3-5 year horizon. Moreover, in models of stochastic volatility, such as *Hull and White* (1987), it is typically assumed that volatility is mean reverting. ARCH models tend to outperform other models in forecasting volatility. In particular, ARCH models have a more flexible and reasonable forecast function than historical volatilities. The forecasts derived from historical volatilities estimates are constant for the whole forecast horizon.

Anomalies

There are several anomalies in literature on which hedge funds can take profits. One of the first papers on long-term return anomalies is *DeBondt and Thaler* (1985). They find that when stocks are ranked on three- to five-year past returns, past winners tend to be future losers, and vice versa.

More recent is the momentum effect identified by *Jegadeesh and Titman* (1993); stocks with high returns over the past year tend to have high returns over the following three to six months.

Lakonishok et al. (1994) argue that ratios involving stock prices proxy for past performance. Firms with high ratios of earnings to price (E/P), cash flow to price (C/P), and book-to-market equity (BE/ME) tend to have poor past earnings growth, and firms with low E/P, C/P, and BE/ME tend to have strong past earnings growth. Because the market over-reacts to past growth, it is surprised when earnings growth mean reverts. As a result, high E/P, C/P, and

BE/ME stocks (poor past performers) have high future returns, and low E/P, C/P, and BE/ME stocks (strong past performers) have low future returns.

Ritter (1991) and *Loughran and Ritter* (1995) classify the poor long-term post-event returns of initial public offerings and seasoned equity offerings. *Mitchell and Stafford* (1997) show that seasoned equity offerings have strong stock returns in the three years prior to the issue.

Asquith (1983) and *Agrawal et al.* (1992) find negative long-term abnormal returns to acquiring firms following mergers. This might be attributed to market underreaction to a poor investment decision (Roll (1986)) or overreaction to the typically strong performance of acquiring firms in advance of mergers, documented in *Mitchell and Stafford* (1997).

Ikenberry and Lakonishok (1993) find negative post-event abnormal returns for firms involved in proxy contests.

Lakonishok and Vermaelen (1990) find positive long-term post-event abnormal returns when firms tender for their stock. *Ikenberry et al.* (1995) observe similar results for open-market share repurchases argued that the long-term negative post-listing abnormal stock returns of firms that newly list on the NYSE or Amex are due to overreaction (Dharan and Ikenberry (1995)).

Cusatis et al. (1993) find positive post-event abnormal returns for divesting firms and the firms they divest. They attribute the result to market underreaction to an enhanced probability that, after a spinoff, both the parent and the spinoff are likely to become merger targets, and the recipients of premiums. *Desai and Jain* (1997) and *Ikenberry et al.* (1996) find that split their stock experience long-term positive abnormal returns both before and after the split.

Evidence that stock prices seem to respond to earnings for about a year after they are announced can be found in *Ball and Brown* (1968) and *Bernard and Thomas* (1990).

Shiller (1984) found that irrational investor behaviour resulted in excess bond and stock market volatility.

Technical Analysis

Technical analysis involves searching for recurrent and predictable patterns in stock prices. This type of analysis has a long history and dates back to the Japanese rice traders trading on the Dojima Rice Exchange in Osaka as early as the 1600s.

According to *Cheung and Wong* (1999), 25 to 30 percent of the foreign exchange dealers base most of their trade on technical trading signals.

Technical analysis is primarily visual, while quantitative finance is primarily algebraic and numerical. Popular patterns of traditional technical analysis are listed by *Edwards and Magee* (1966). Patterns have been studied, among others, by *Levy* (1971), Osler (1998), *Dempster and Jones* (1998), *Chang and Osler* (1999) and *Lo, Mamaysky, and Wang* (2000) who have mainly focused on the profitability of trading rules related to chart patterns and also on the informational content that could generate such patterns. Direct support has been given by *Pruitt and White* (1988), *Neftci* (1991*), Broth, Lakonishok, and LeBaron* (1992), *Neely, Weber and Dittmar* (1997), *Neely and Weller* (1998), *Chang and Osler* (1994), *Osler and Chang* (1995), and *Allen and Karjalainen* (1999).

All these investigations conclude to the lack of profitability of these technical patterns. However, *Lo, Mamaysky, and Wang* (2000) find that these patterns present an informational content that affect stock returns. *Murphy* (1999) and *Bechu and Bertrand* (1999), argue that patterns present a predictive success which allows traders to acquire profit by developing specific trading rules. Since the seminal work of *Friedman* (1953) and *Fama* (1970), the role of technical analysis as a forecasting mechanism continues to remain controversial in the literature.

Brock, Lakonishok, and LeBaron (1992) support the use of two of the simplest and most popular trading rules: moving average and trading range break. They show that these trading rules help to predict return variations in the Dow Jones index.

In fact, one finds again and again that more sophisticated models are superior in in-sample comparisons but these models are often outperformed in out-of-sample forecasts by simpler and more robust models. The prime example is presumably the random-walk model which, despite its simplicity, is often difficult to beat in forecasting contests.

4.2 Principles of Garch

If an autoregressive moving average model is assumed for the error variance, the model is a generalized autoregressive conditional heteroskedasticity model after *Bollerslev* (1986).

$$\sigma^2 = \gamma V + \alpha u^2{}_{n-1} + \beta \sigma^2{}_{n-1} \qquad (29)$$

where the parameters are set to α=0,13, λ=0,94 and β=0,86 after RiskMetrics by *J.P.Morgan* (1997). The new volatility is measured by a long run component γV, today's volatility $u^2{}_{n-1}$ and the old estimate $\sigma^2{}_{n-1}$.

There are several specifications in Garch models. For example the NGarch by *Engle and Ng* (1993), EGARCH model by *Nelson* (1991), GARCH-M, QGARCH model by *Sentana* (1995), GJR-GARCH model by *Glosten, Jagannathan and Runkle*(1993), TGARCH model by *Zakoian* (1994), fGARCH by Hentschel's (1995) and many more. Specifications are made on conditional standard deviation instead of conditional variance, the residual process, adding a heteroskedasticity term into the mean equation or nonlinear asymmetric fitting.

For performance of GARCH models please read *West, Edison and Cho* (1993), for non-linear trading rules *Satchell and Timmermann* (1995) and on return predictability *Kandel and Stambaugh* (1996).

Noh, Engle and Kane (1994) examine the profitability of a straddle strategy derived from a GARCH model against forecasts from autoregressive models based on implied volatilities. The GARCH model turns out to provide the superior strategy.

Multi Asset Applicability

The main result that option trading strategies based on GARCH models, produce significant and superior profitability is also confirmed by *Kang and Brorsen* (1995) for options on wheat futures and by *Kroner and Levin* (1996) for foreign currency options.

Chapter Conclusion

As we can find arbitrage possibilities in the market, statistical arbitrage should be possible. Furthermore time series analysis gives a profound edge on performance. Not only does behavioural finance argue in favour of anomalies, but also models like the Garch model achieve returns by algorithmic trading. There have been many adjustments to the Garch model in literature until today. In the next chapter I am going to introduce a semi-variance-model and compare Garch to it. It is important to remember that chart patterns imply the trend of momentum and moving average effects. Those are mostly calculated by open, high, low or close quotes and are verified to supply statistical arbitrage opportunities.

4.3 Introduction of a Semi -Variance Model

Introduction of the Model

The ultimate way to evaluate a model is its usefulness as a tool in many areas such as derivative products pricing, risk evaluation and hedging, portfolio allocation, and the derivation of Value at Risk measures. Thereby the return created by the new model has to outperform the old one. Only a better fit to the input data is not a good indicator for future performance itself. In particular, the measure of volatility chosen in this paper is a second order lower partial moment. Such a measure was also used by *Markowitz* (1959) in his earlier work on the construction of portfolios for loss-averse investors. Markowitz used the term semi-variance to describe the second order lower partial moment. For risk-averse investors, solving for optimal portfolio allocations by minimizing semi-variance would limit the likelihood of a large loss.

$$Semi-Variance = \frac{1}{n} * \sum_{r_t < \mu} (\mu - r_t)^2 \tag{30}$$

where n is the total number of observations below the mean, r_t is the observed value and the mean μ or target value of the data set .

Semi-variance is similar to variance; however, it only considers observations below the mean. It is a useful tool in portfolio or asset analysis, semi-variance provides a measure for downside risk. While standard deviation and variance provide measures of volatility, semi-variance only looks at the negative fluctuations of an asset. By neutralizing all values above the mean, or an investor's target return, semi-variance estimates the average loss that a portfolio could incur. This very important fact gets implemented in the model at the next step.

4.3.1 Methodology

In the semi-variance model, historical data are analyzed to predict future market movements. The model does not only calculate the expected price movement in the next 30 days, but it also gives a prediction of the future confidence interval of investment returns. The model can be applied to stocks, commodities, indices, currencies and every other asset with volatility, but not to bonds as they converge to their nominal value at maturity and thus their volatility decreases. See *Ho and Lee* (1986) or *Cox, Ingersoll and Ross* (1985) for bond models.

Method

In order to generate a profitable model for daily trading, times series analysis and chart pattern detection is used. The huge database generated by this chart patterns lead to the consideration of including all available patterns up to a 30 day trading period. The time series of daily open, high, low, and close quotes are coded into numerical values of ones and zeros.

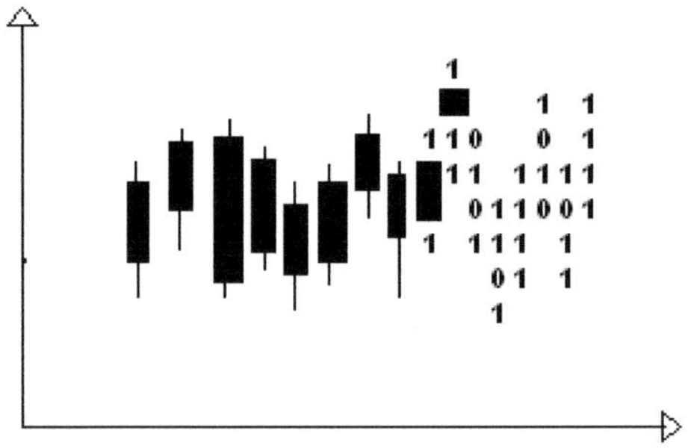

Figure 3

Therefore the open, high, low and close quotes are set in an order. A two day chart pattern delivers 2^8 combinations of possible open, high, low, and close combinations. Those combinations are screened over the historical data set. In every case a combination occurs the following performance is listed and evaluated for variance and semi-variance. Most important is the denotation of semi-variance into the database, because it will deliver very important information for the Value at Risk procedure later. In the next step two more sequential days are set into relation to the first day. This step can be repeated as often as necessary to create a digital picture of the chart pattern. For every new day in the sample, a higher quality result can be generated. The prediction power will increase with further days added. The used DAX sample covers a little more than 4800 days. The actual chart patterns start from one day patterns up to 30 day patterns. After generating the patterns and checking the historical data for its occurrence, the performance analysis is done. The most important feature of the computer algorithm is in fact, that not all chart patterns are calculated upfront, but only the given patterns in the historical data are used. This reduces the database memory by far and no mathematical combinatorial functions are necessary. The 30 day returns are listed according their chart pattern. For every new return series the average return is recalculated and the according semi-variance recorded. In the case of out-of-sample prediction the chart pattern code can be looked up in the list and prediction for the return and the higher moment variances can be displayed.

4.3.2 Description of Market Data

Foundation of the historical time series analysis has been the DAX – „Deutscher Aktien Index" of the Deutsche Börse AG. This index contains the 30 largest German stocks and is traded in Frankfurt am Main. The times series is split into two different parts: Namely 26.11.1990 to 21.8.2008 as part one and 21.8.2008 to 15.4.2010 as part two. Part one is used as in-sample for training and testing the semi-variance-model. Part two from 21.8.2008 to 15.4.210 is the out-of-sample period for a direct backtest with real options data.

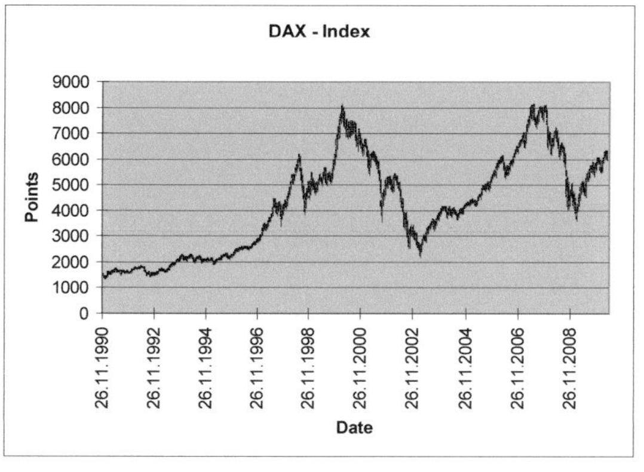

Figure 4

Analyzing the performance by a *Jarque and Bera* test, gives evidence about the normal distribution of returns. A *Jarque and Bera* test value below 0,6218 indicates a normal distribution of returns. The lowest test value has been 59,42 for the 4 day returns at 5% significance level. Thus we can strongly neglect the fact that returns are normal distributed in the time period from one up to 30 days in the testing period.

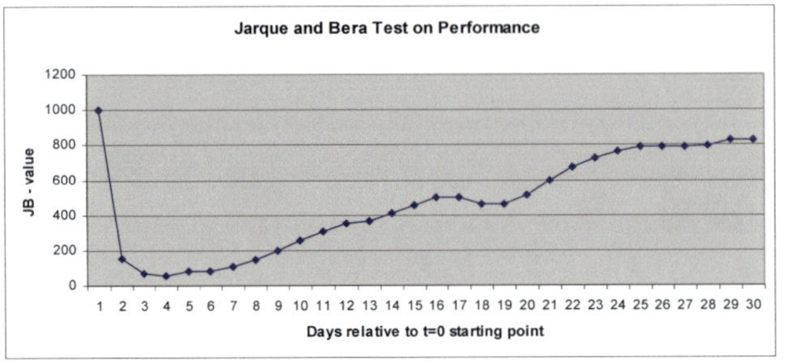

Figure 5

The Jarque and Bera test is calculated by:

$$JB_i = \frac{T}{6} * (S_i^{\ 2} + \frac{1}{4} * E_i^{\ 2}) \tag{31}$$

where T is time, S_i is the skew and E_i equals excess.

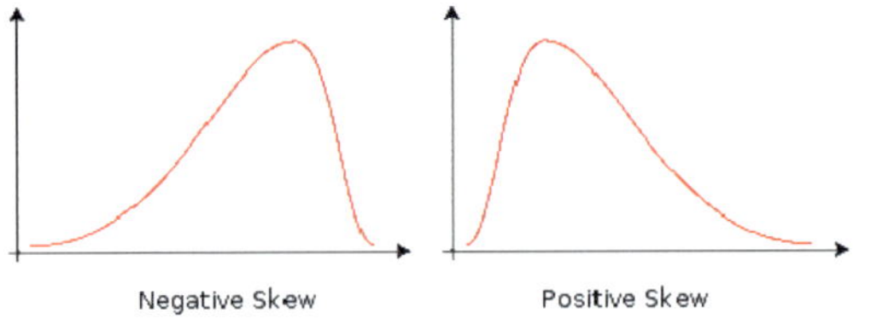

Figure 6

A negative skew indicates a distribution's shift to the right. This can be helpful in the case of downward risk-averse investors. Our data sample has been strongly negative in skew. Taking this skew into account and also taking care of the kurtosis we get different results. In our 20 day horizon the DAX had a negative skewness of -0,57 with an average performance of 0,78% and a non normal distributed JB-ratio of 513,34. The Garch standard deviation of 6,25% exceeded the semi-variance-approach in both directions.

Examining the DAX distribution on higher moments, we find the following chart of short term returns:

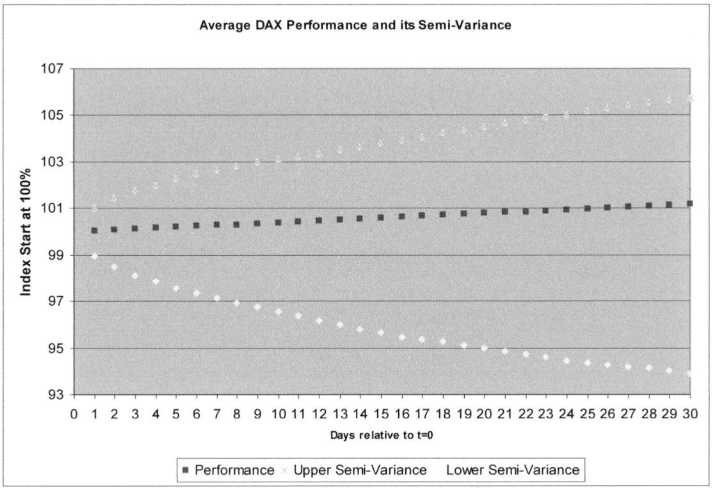

Figure 7

The performance slowly rises and has a positive slope. The upper semi-variance ascends slower than the lower semi-variance falls. There is more volatility to the bottom than to the top. Data from emerging market countries provide a particularly interesting illustration as the use of semi-variance as a measure of risk is most efficient when the conditional distribution of returns is skewed (Bond and Satchell (2002)).

4.3.3 Prediction Power

Comparing the model to the actual realized DAX returns we can find the following results: The accuracy of the mean prediction compared to the actual DAX realization is roughly plus minus 5%. The figure below shows the exact error spread from the actual value as an index with a start value of one.

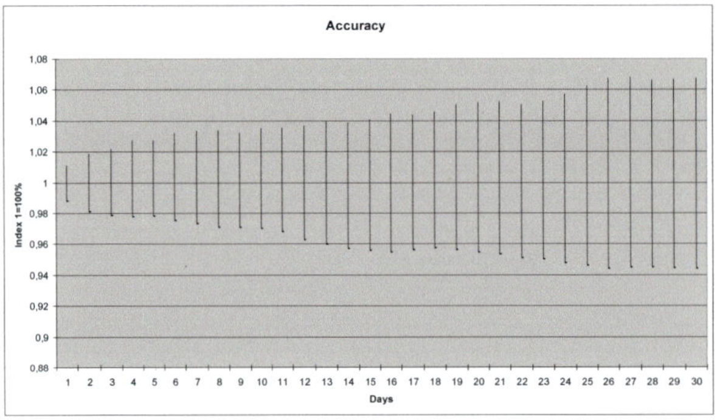

Figure 8

An example of the predictions by Garch and the semi-variance-model are displayed below. As the Garch model only relies on the last recent quote and the volatility, we can find a quite different picture for the semi-variance-model.

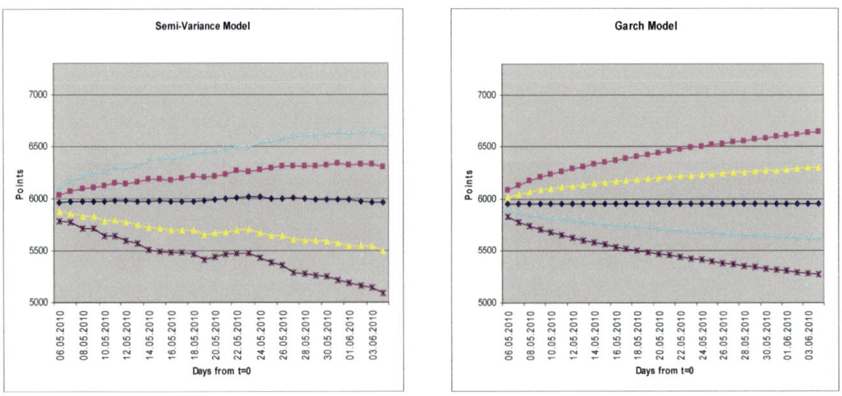

Figure 9

4.3.4 Risk Measurement

Value at Risk

Taking different market situations into account, also the standard deviations change. The entire backtest data has been classified into different market trends. The realized DAX standard deviation has been 3,89% in a rising market and 8,37% in a falling market. Under nearly stable conditions the standard deviation has been at around 4,05%. The necessary deviation for a 5% Value at Risk gives the following findings: Garch predicts a higher deviation in bull markets and a lower deviation in bear markets. The semi-variance-model implies much higher deviations, which we can read in the table above. The spread to Garch is much higher. By "spread" we classify the difference between the standard deviation of Garch multiplied by two and the sum of the upper and absolute lower semi-variance of the new model. In the bear market from 7.1.2008-2.3.2009 the difference of spread's has been at 20,58%, whereas in a moderate market from 27.11.90-16.9.96 a negative spread difference of -0,43% has been occurred.

VaR(5%; 20 day)	Bull Market 2003/03/09- 2007/05/25	Bear Market 2008/01/07- 2009/03/02	Moderate Market 1990/11/27- 1996/09/16	All Time Data 1990/11/26- 2010/05/05
DAX Standart Deviation	3,86	8,37	4,05	6,11
Garch Standart Deviation	4,87	7,24	6,33	6,23
Semi-Variance -Model				
Upper Semi-Variance	7,9292	15,6154	5,5753	8,1168
Lower Semi-Variance	-5,5332	-19,4535	-6,64746	-9,48039
Spread	3,7224	20,5889	-0,43724	5,13719

Table 2

Shortfall

The 5% VaR shortfall is slightly higher for the semi-variance-model. Especially the lower -13,17% shortfall exceeds the Garch model's shortfall by 0,47%. This fact can be reduced to a larger quantile of shortfalls in the Garch model and thus a higher density below the standard deviation calculated.

Shortfall at 5% VaR (1990-2010; 20day)	Upper	Lower
Garch	9,647485164	12,70509
Semi-Variance -Model	11,06788949	13,17126

Table 3

4.4 Backtest with Real Options

The intention is to set up a model with lower risk, but higher return at the same Value-at-Risk. The portfolio is constructed by a call- and an put spread at the same time.

The DAX predicted volatility by both models is separately traded in a one year time horizon with 12 trades per year. This is because the options lose most of their time value in the last 20 days of trading. The option strikes are chosen by the given volatility risk. The variance and also the semi-variance have been multiplied by a factor until to a given percentage of shortfall. A 0% Vale at Risk is chosen for the lower call strike and the upper put strike. Both options are traded long. A 0% Value at Rsik means, that no deviation exceeds the quantile in the historical data, but this is no guarantee for the future accuracy. A 1% Value at Risk is chosen for the short options with closer strike to the actual quote. In the figure below you can see the time dependent strategy

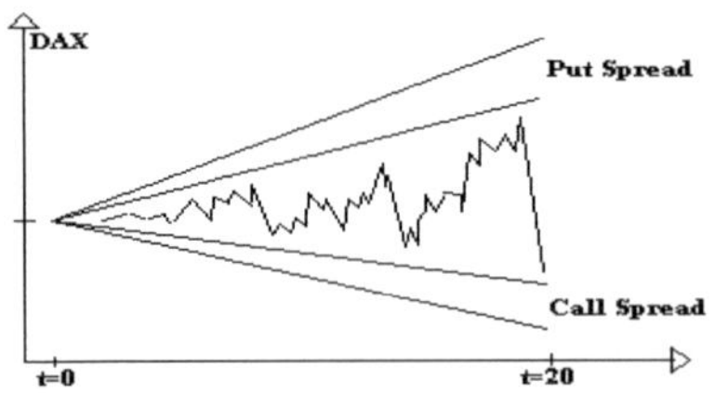

Figure 10

This strategy is not a clear market neutral strategy, because the delta of both spreads does not sum up to zero. In fact it has to be hedged by an additional future contract. The hedge is not performed in this analysis, since the advantages of a semi-variance model should be shown and no hedge would be necessary, if the prediction was right in the end. There are many more delta neutral option strategies (straddles, strangles, etc.) which could be alternatively used for the backtest. The described strategy has the following payoff diagram:

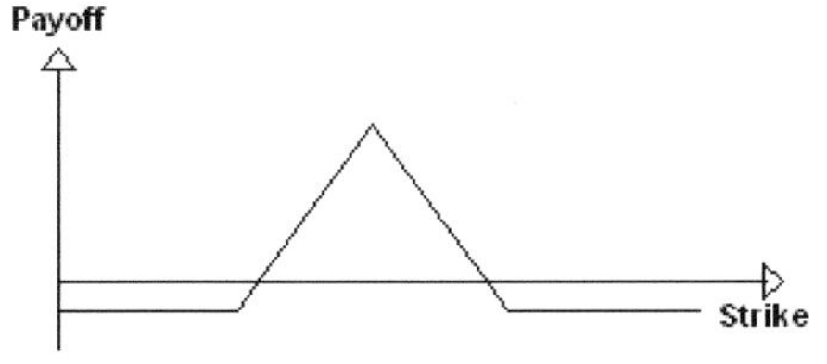

Figure 11

4.4.1 Out-of-Sample Market Data

The out-of-sample backtest has been conducted in the time frame from 2008/08/21 to 2009/04/15. This market phase has been characterized by a steep downward movement in the first place and a correction in the second phase. Thus it is the optimal environment of high volatility and changes in market trends.

A detailed table with all traded instruments is listed in the Appendix. All option data can be found online in the *BNP Paribas* (2010) database for expired options. As further price time series were necessary the *Euwax* (2010) provides these information on its website. As a very important issue the strategy is designed to be reimplemented also by private investors trough a new product category of "discount options". These certificates are similar to call or put option spreads. For this reason I used options emitted by BNP Paribas, instead of options traded directly at the exchange. By focusing only on one issuer, fewer options were available. Not every trade could be conducted, because of missing option strike prices. Consequently only the strategies were executed, which could be implemented in both models. The purpose of verifying the semi-variance-model's outperformance as compared with the Garch model is not affected, since only in the case of availability for both models the trades were recorded.

Furthermore not every private investor feels sophisticated enough to control risk management associated with option writing, but he is certainly less risk averse to buy discount option products. This decision infects bid/ask spreads as well as the option prices. Normally emitters charge a premium to justify by the expenses in issuing a new certificate. This procedure does not infect the backtest results. Especially because the focus is set on verifying a superior performance of a semi-variance model, compared to Garch model. As a result the bid ask spread is not relevant for the comparison of the two models, only the ask quote has been analyzed regarding its price change. Again the analysis is not meant to show the trading strategies profitability itself, but the difference in models. Therefore also an one month rolling buy and hold strategy of direct investment in the DAX-Index has been added.

4.4.2 Performance Comparison

Performance measurement can be difficult. Hedge funds try to aim low volatility. They can provide small returns, but with volatility close to zero they can have a great sharpe-ratios. *Eling (2006)* reports that most of the performance measurement ratios show the same result as the sharpe-ratio. This supports easy decision making.

At first sight the return of semi-variance-models has been 2,56% and thus 1,86% higher than in the Garch model. DAX delivers 1,01% with an standard deviation of 8,86%. Whereas Garch has a lower standard deviation of 6,07%, the semi-variance-model can top that by 1,49%. Thus the sharpe-ratio of 1,57 in the semi-variance-model is by far higher than the 0,097 ratio by Garch and 0,09 of DAX. This is first evident of superior return. Moreover the Value at Risk (5%) is only at -5,01% in the semi-variance-model, while -10,78% at Garch. Garch actually has a higher Vale at Risk than the -9,61% DAX investment it self, but the expected shortfall of -9,64% is 4,7% is lower than DAX. There has been no expected shortfall in the semi-variance-model. The maximum drawdown has been -21,15% for Dax and -17,58% in Garch. On average the drawdown has been -6,69% for DAX in the given 20 day horizon and 17,58% in Garch.

As opposed to this, all returns in the semi-variance model have been positive and larger than the risk-free rate.

Omega, Sortio-ratio, Kapp3 and upside-potential-ratio have been better for the Garch model compared to DAX, this is due to the lower-partial-moment. On the other hand the lower expected return, but a high maximum drawdown let the Calmar-ratio drop below DAX. The Sterling- and Burke-ratio show the expected outperformance, since the average drawdown of Garch has been better than DAX. As there is a lower-partial-moment of zero for the semi-variance, not only the Calmar-, Sterling-, and Burke-ratio are zero, but also the Omega, Sortino-, Kappa3, upside-potential-ratio and the conditional sharpe-ratio. This makes a comparison very difficult. The ratios show a clear outperformance of Garch compared to the DAX buy and hold strategy. Additionally the semi-variance-model performs better than

Garch in respect to sharp-ratio and drawdown. Thus we can conclude that the semi-variance-model outperforms the Garch model.

This conclusion becomes clearer taking a closer look to Excess Return on Value at Risk, Conditional sharpe-ratio and Modified sharpe-ratio. The semi-variance has the smallest Value at Risk, no shortfall recorded and a thin kurtosis. All three ratios state the outperformance of the semi-variance-model opposed to Garch and DAX.

Performance Measures	Semi-Variance-Model	Garch	DAX one Month rolling buy and hold
Sharpe-Ratio	1,575681137	0,096956	0,089879
Expected return per month	2,56%	0,80%	1,01%
Standart deviation	1,49%	6,07%	8,86%
Return per annum	31,98%	7,62%	9,09%
VaR(5%;20day)	-5,01%	-10,78%	-9,61%
Shortfall %	0%	-9,64%	-14,34%
Maximum Drawdown	0%	-17,58%	-21,15%
Average Drawdown	0%	-17,58%	-6,69%
Skew	0,479762115	-2,84448	-1,13841
Kurtosis	0,118357732	8,938164	2,290838
JB-Ratio	3,843562044	30,99531	3,080361
Omega	0	0,392578	0,23072
Sortino-Ratio	0	0,021796	0,006028
Kappa 3	0	0,00121	0,000145
Upside-Potential-Ratio	0	0,402003	0,268665
Calmar-Ratio	0	0,033502	0,037677
Sterling-Ratio	0	0,033502	0,119005
Burke-Ratio	0	0,001905	0,000493
Excess Return on Value at Risk	0,4686	0,06374	0,082871
Conditional Sharpe-Ratio	0	0,061077	0,055584
Modified Sharpe Ratio	0,443539107	0,139268	0,063075

Table 4

5.1 Conclusion

In chapter one, an overview of the different hedge fund strategies is given and the different strategies explained, then performance measures to compare different approaches are introduced. This is especially relevant for the portfolio selection process. Every investor needs means to compare the return he earns with an specific investment to the risk in different projects and has to balance against.

In the second part the theory of statistical arbitrage is introduced in detail. To build a model on this foundation, many market anomalies were presented. At least some of those anomalies can be exploited by technical analysis. Picking the best models for chart pattern analysis and accepting the random walk of asset prices at the same time, delivered a synoptic approach – the semi-variance-model. The idea of a computer based prediction model was born. Because of the existent models for volatility forecasting, the semi-variance-model is compared to the standard Garch model. As the previously defined performance measure were concerned, the semi-variance-model allows for a smaller kurtosis risk. Under the presumption of this insight, an option model is build around the DAX forecast. This forecast was backtested over the last two years and showed a much higher return risk balance than the Garch model. Also many other performance measures displayed the same result of outperformance. Because in statistical arbitrage the model is mostly based on historical data there is still no clear evidence for the correctness of the semi-variance-model. There has to be done more research on this topic.

5.2 Further Research

There are many areas of further research. The model can be expanded in various ways. Not only does the market provide ignored statistical arbitrage opportunities, which have to be discovered by more sophisticated computer algorithms, but also the structure of the model itself can be optimized. In the following I am going to present various ways to improvement:

Expanding the Model

It would be possible to further expand the semi-variance-model according to the maximum drawdown method. In this case the recording of semi-variances could also be upgraded by maximum outliers. Over a very long horizon of time, there could be the convergence to a risk-free model. If call option strikes were set below the 0% VaR a total loss would be considered impossible.

Hedging the Model

A clear statistical arbitrage strategy is characterized by market neutrality. To reach this target delta hedging is necessary. Our usage of a call- and put spread at the same time does take account of this phenomenon partially, but not to the full extend. The call spread's remaining long delta is not fully offset by the put spread's short delta. This is due to the shift in strikes away from the normal distribution and the market's different expectations at each time. This problem can be solved by using future or forward contracts. If the portfolio shows a positive delta, a future short can neutralize the market exposure. A market movement in the opposite direction of delta would therefore be neutralized and the portfolio has an overall beta of zero. In a large portfolio of many assets, a delta hedge could be implemented by calculating the portfolio's beta. This is done by combining the beta of all assets and then hedging only the portfolios beta accordingly with futures.

Technical Analysis Enter and Exit Signals

The model can be enhanced by implementing different additional strategies. Value and momentum strategies have been proven to generate excess return. Further research could show how a combination of those strategies infects return. The option spreads could be traded according to enter and exit signals, which are provided by technical analyses. The Model does not have to be market neutral all the time.

Multi Asset Portfolio or "how not to put all eggs in one basket"

Appling the model to a portfolio with a large number of contained assets improves the sharpe ratio. This is due to diversification effects. The model could calculate the strike prices for all options implied and again a delta hedge can be added. The combination of assets reduces the risk of one single shortfall. Hereby the database would have to be updated with the historical time series of all assets and thus creating a very large database. Decisions for reducing this database are necessary.

Change of Underlying

Our approach can be extended in various directions. Most obviously, it can be applied to other markets than equities like currencies or commodities. Furthermore it would also be interesting to backtest other option trading strategies such as butterflies, condors, and strangles.

6.1 List of Literature

Agrawal, A., Jaffe, Mandelker, G. (1992), The post-merger performance of acquiring Firms: a reexamination of an anomaly. Journal of Finance, 47, pp. 1605-1621

Agrarwal, V. and Naik, N. (2000), Multi-period Performance Persistence Analysis of Hedge Funds, Journal of Finance and Quantitative Analysis, 35, 3, pp. 327-342

Allen, F. and Karjalainen, R. (1999), Using Genetic Algorithms to Find Technical Trading Rules", Journal of Financial Economics 51, pp. 245-271.

Asquith, P. (1983), Merger bids, uncertainty and stockholder returns. Journal of Financial Economics, 11, pp. 51-83.

Ball, R., Brown, P. (1968), An empirical evaluation of accounting income numbers. Journal of Accounting Research 6, pp. 159-178.

Bechu, T., and E. Bertrand (1999), L'analyse technique: pratiques et mthodes, gestion. Economica.

Bernard, V., Thomas, J. (1990), Evidence that stock prices do not fully reflect the implications of current earnings for future earnings, Journal of Accounting and Economics, 13, p. 305.

Bondarenko, Oleg (2003), The Review of Financial Studies, Vol. 16, No. 3 (Autumn, 2003), pp. 875-919

Bond, S.A. (1999), Time Varying Skewness and Downside Risk Measurement: A Comparison of Models, paper presented to the Royal Economic Society Annual Conference, March-April 1999, University of Nottingham, Nottingham.

Bond, S.A. and Satchell, S.E. (2002) 'Statistical Properties of the Sample Semi-variance', Applied Mathematical Finance, 9, pp 219-239.

Bollerslev, Tim (1986), Generalized Autoregressive Conditional Heteroscedasticity. Journal of Econometrics, Vol. 31, pp. 307-327.

Brock, W., Lakonishok, J. and LeBaron, B. (1992), Simple Technical Trading Rules and the Stochastic Properties of Stock Returns, Journal of Finance, 47, pp. 1731-1764.

Chan, Louis, Jegadeesh, Narasimhan and Joseph Lakonishok (1996), Momentum strategies, Journal of Finance, 51, pp. 1681—1713.

Chang, K. and C. Osler (1994), Evaluating Chart-Based Technical Analysis: The Headand-Shoulders Pattern in Foreign Exchange Markets", working paper, Federal Reserve Bank of New York.

Chang, P., and C. Osler (1999), Methodical madness: technical analysis and the irrationality of exchange-rate forecasts," The Economic Journal, 109, pp. 636–661.

Chordia, T., R. Roll, and A. Subrahmanyam (2002), Evidence on the speed of Convergence to Market Efficiency," UCLA Working paper.

Cusatis, P., Miles, J., Woolridge, J. (1993), Restructuring through spinoffs, Journal of Financial Economics 33, pp. 293-311.

Dharan, B., Ikenberry, D. (1995), The long-run negative drift of post-listing stock returns. Journal of Finance, 50, pp. 1547-1574.

DeBondt, W., Thaler, R. (1985), Does the stock market overreact? Journal of Finance, 40, pp. 793-805.

Desai, H., Jain, P. (1997), Long-run common stock returns following splits and reverse splits. Journal of Business, 70, pp. 409-433.

Edwards, Robert and John Magee (1966), Technical Analysis of Stock Trends, 5th Edition (John Magee Inc., Boston, MA).

Eling, Martin (2006), Hedgefonds-Strategien und ihre Performance. Finanzierung, Kapitalmarkt und Banken. Lohmar : Eul-Verlag, 2006

Fama, E. and Blume, M. (1966) Filter rules and stock market trading profits. Journal of Business, 39, pp. 226–41.

Fama, Eugene F (1970), Efficient Capital Markets: A Review of Theory and Empirical Work, Journal of Finance, 25, May, pp. 383-417.

Fama, Eugene F. (1997), Market Efficiency, Long-Term Returns, and Behavioral Finance, Available at SSRN: http://ssrn.com/abstract=15108

Hogan, S., Jarrow, R., Teo, M. and M. Warachka (2003), Testing Market Efficiency using Statistical Arbitrage with Applications to Momentum and Value Strategies, Credit Suisse First Boston, Johnson Graduate School of Management, Singapore Management University September, 2003

Hull, J.C.(2009), Options, Futures, and Other Derivatives, Prentice Hall.

Ikenberry, D., Lakonishok, J. (1993), Corporate governance through the proxy contest: evidence and implications. Journal of Business, 66, pp.405-435.

Ikenberry, D., Lakonishok, J., Vermaelen, T. (1995), Market underreaction to open market share repurchases. Journal of Financial Economics, 39, pp. 181-208.

Indjic, D. and A. Heen (2003), AIMA Survey of Hedge Fund Classification Practice, AIMA Journal, Sept.

Jarrow, Robert A., Hogan, Steve, Teo, Melvyn and Warachka, Mitch (2003), Testing Market Efficiency Using Statistical Arbitrage with Applications to Momentum and Value Strategies (April 15, 2003)

Jegadeesh, Narasimhan and Sheridan Titman (1993), Returns to buying winners and selling losers: Implications for stock market efficiency, Journal of Finance, 48,
pp. 65-91.

Jensen, B.C. and Bennington, G.A. (1970), "Random Walk and Technical Theories: Some Additional Evidence", Journal of Finance, 25, pp. 469-482.

J. P. Morgan (1997), RiskMetrics, Technical Documents, 4th Edition. New York.

Lakonishok, J., Shleifer, A., Vishny, R.(1994), Contrarian investment, extrapolation, and risk. Journal of Finance, 49, pp. 1541-1578.

Levy, R. (1971), The predictive significance of five-point patterns. Journal of Business, 41, pp. 316–323.

Kaiser, Dieter G (2003), Hedgefonds : Entmystifizierung einer Anlageklasse ; Strukturen - Chancen - Risiken / Dieter G. Kaiser. - 1. Aufl. - Wiesbaden : Gabler, 2003.

Lo, A.W., H. Mamaysky, and J. Wang (2000), "Foundations of Technical Analysis: Computational Algorithms, Statistical Inference, and Empirical Implementation," Journal of Finance, 55, pp. 1075-765.

Malkiel, Burton (1996), A Random Walk Down Wall Street: Including a Life-Cycle Guide to Personal Investing (W.W. Norton, New York, NY).

Markowitz, H.M. (1959), Portfolio Selection: Efficient Diversification of Investments, John Wiley and Sons, New York.

Murphy, J. (1999), Technical analysis of the financial markets. New York Institute of Finance.

Natenberg,S. (1994), Option Volatility and Pricing Strategies: Advanced Trading Techniques for Professionals McGraw-Hill Professional Publishing.

Neftci, S. (1991), Naive Trading Rules in Financial Markets and Wiener--Kolmogorov Prediction Theory: A Study of Technical Analysis", Journal of Business 64, pp. 549- 571.

Neely, C.,Weller, P. and R. Dittmar (1997), Is Technical Analysis in the Foreign Exchange Market Profitable? A Genetic Programming Approach", Journal of Financial and Quantitative Analysis 32, pp. 405-426.

Neely, C. and P. Weller (1998), Technical Trading Rules in the European Monetary System", working paper, Federal Bank of St. Louis.

Nelson, D. B. (1991), Conditional heteroskedasticity in asset returns: A new approach, Econometrica 59, pp. 347-370.

Osler, C. and K. Chang, (1995), Head and Shoulders: Not Just a Flaky Pattern., Staff Report No. 4, Federal Reserve Bank of New York.

Pruitt, Stephen and Robert White (1988), The CRISMA trading system: Who says technical analysis can't beat the market?, Journal of Portfolio Management, 14, pp. 55-58.

Roll, R. (1986), The hubris hypothesis of corporate takeovers, Journal of Business 59, pp. 197-216.

Rogers, L.C.G., and S.E. Satchell (1991), "Estimating Variance from High, Low and Closing Prices,"Annals of Applied Probability, 1, pp. 504-512.

Sharpe, W. F. (1994), The Sharpe ratio. J. Portfolio Management, 21, 1, pp. 49-58

Shiller, R.J. (1987), Investor Behaviour in the October 1987 Stock Market Crash: Survey Evidence, NBER Working Paper, No. 2446. Reprinted in Market Volatility, MIT Press.

Sullivan, R., Timmermann, A. and White, H. (1999), "Data-snooping, Technical Trading Rule Performance, and the Bootstrap", Journal of Finance, 54, pp. 1647-1691.

Internet Sources

Absolute-Report (2010),
Content description: Performance of hedge fund indices,
[http://www.absolut-report.de/ap/26 , found at 2010/05/05]

BAFIN (2010),
Content description: Bafin on hedge fund regulation,
[http://www.bafin.de/cln_171/nn_724052/DE/Unternehmen/Fonds/Hedgefonds/hedgefonds__node.html?__nnn=true , found at 2010/05/16]

BNP Paribas (2010),
Content description: Overview of expired call- and put options,
[http://www.derivate.bnpparibas.com/DE/index.aspx?pageID=36 , found at 2010/05/10]

CSFB (2009),
Content description: Industry review
[http://www.hedgeindex.com/hedgeindex/documents/CS%20Tremont%202009%20Industry%20Review%20v8.pdf , found at 2010/05/10]

CSFB(2010)
Content description: Overview hedge fund strategy performances
[http://www.hedgeindex.com/hedgeindex/en/indexoverview.aspx?indexname=HEDG&cy=USD , found at 2010/05/10]

Euwax (2010),
Content description: Database for historical prices of expired options,
[https://www.boerse-stuttgart.de/de/toolsundservices/euwaxarchiv/gesamt-archiv.html , found at 2010/05/10]

EFAMA (2005),
Content description: EFAMA on hedge fund regulation in europe - a comparative survey (November 2005),

http://www.efama.org/index.php?option=com_docman&task=doc_download&gid=176&Itemid=-99 , found at 2010/05/16]

EFAMA (2006),
Content description: Principles of taxation on UCITS
[http://www.efama.org/index.php?option=com_docman&task=doc_download&gid=16&Itemid=-99 , p. 22, found at 2010/05/16]

HFR(2010)
Content description: Hedge fund style classification
[https://www.hedgefundresearch.com/index.php?fuse=hfrx_strats&1274397730 , found at 2010/05/19]

Market Folly(2010)
Content descipton: World's largest hedge funds
[http://www.marketfolly.com/2010/03/worlds-largest-hedge-funds.html. found at 2010/05/15]

6.2 Appendix

This table shows the traded options for the model proof.

Semi-Variance Model									
Options bought					Options sold				
	Call	Call	Put	Put		Call	Call	Put	Put
	long	short	short	long		long	short	short	long
	Price in T=0					Price in T=1			
17.03.2010	11,21	10,21			15.04.2010	13,94	12,94		
18.02.2010	9,26	8,28			18.03.2010	12,91	11,91		
21.01.2010					18.02.2010				
11.12.2009					14.01.2010				
19.11.2009	15,77	13,78	7,32	10,29	17.12.2009	16,84	14,84	6,16	9,16
22.10.2009	10,47	9,49			19.11.2009	9,58	8,58		
17.09.2009	10,43	9,45			15.10.2009	11,23	10,23		
20.08.2009	10,21	9,24			17.09.2009	14,37	13,37		
23.07.2009					20.08.2009				
21.05.2009	11,1	10,13	6,56	7,52	18.06.2009	9,91	8,91	7,59	8,59
14.04.2009	8,83	7,88			12.05.2009	10,28	9,28		
16.03.2009					14.04.2009				
19.02.2009			8,75	9,73	19.03.2009			10,27	11,27
19.01.2009					17.02.2009				
20.11.2008					18.12.2008			1,3	2,3
23.10.2008					20.11.2008				
18.09.2008			6,95	8,87	16.10.2008			20,94	22,94
21.08.2008			8,24	9,21	18.09.2008			9,58	10,58

Garch									
Options bought					Options sold				
	Call	Call	Put	Put		Call	Call	Put	Put
	long	short	short	long		long	short	short	long
	Price in T=0					Price in T=1			
17.03.2010	11,21	10,21			15.04.2010	13,94	12,94		
18.02.2010	10,25	9,26	6,43	8,34	18.03.2010	13,91	12,91	0,06	2,06
21.01.2010					18.02.2010				
11.12.2009					14.01.2010				
19.11.2009	12,29	11,31	6,36	8,31	17.12.2009	13,34	12,34	5,16	7,16
22.10.2009	12,45	11,46			19.11.2009	11,58	10,58		
17.09.2009	11,41	10,43			15.10.2009	12,23	11,23		
20.08.2009	15,15	13,16			17.09.2009	19,37	17,73		
23.07.2009					20.08.2009				
21.05.2009			8,5	12,48	18.06.2009			9,59	13,59
14.04.2009					12.05.2009				
16.03.2009					14.04.2009				
19.02.2009			6,85	9,73	19.03.2009			8,27	11,27

19.01.2009					17.02.2009				
20.11.2008			11,73	16,57	18.12.2008			7,3	12,3
23.10.2008			13,9	18,85	20.11.2008			15,88	20,88
18.09.2008			5,86	8,67	16.10.2008			17,94	20,94
21.08.2008			7,26	9,21	18.09.2008			8,58	10,58

Table 5

Single Hedge Funds registered at Bafin:

http://www.bafin.de/cln_171/SharedDocs/Downloads/DE/Unternehmen/Fonds/Hedgefonds/Sondervermoegen,templateId=raw,property=publicationFile.pdf/Sondervermoegen.pdf

Annualized Return Comparison (January 1994 – December 2009)

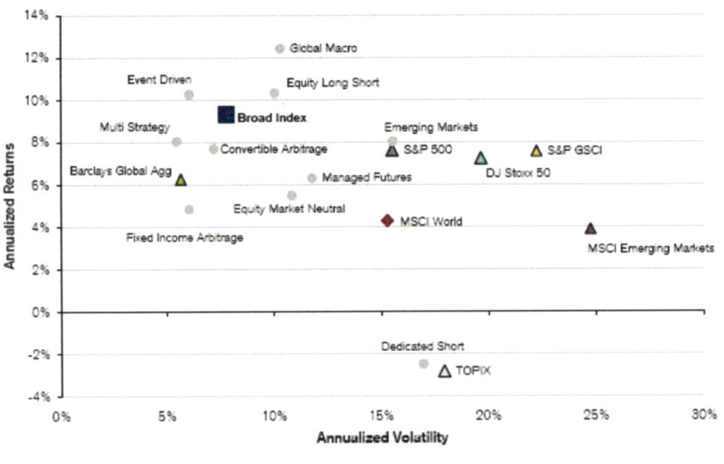

Source: Credit Suisse/Tremont Hedge Fund Index. All data was obtained from internally developed data and other third party sources believed to be reliable. Credit Suisse has not sought to independently verify information obtained from public and third party sources and makes no representations or warranties as to accuracy, completeness or reliability of such information. Please refer to endnotes for index definitions.

Figure 12

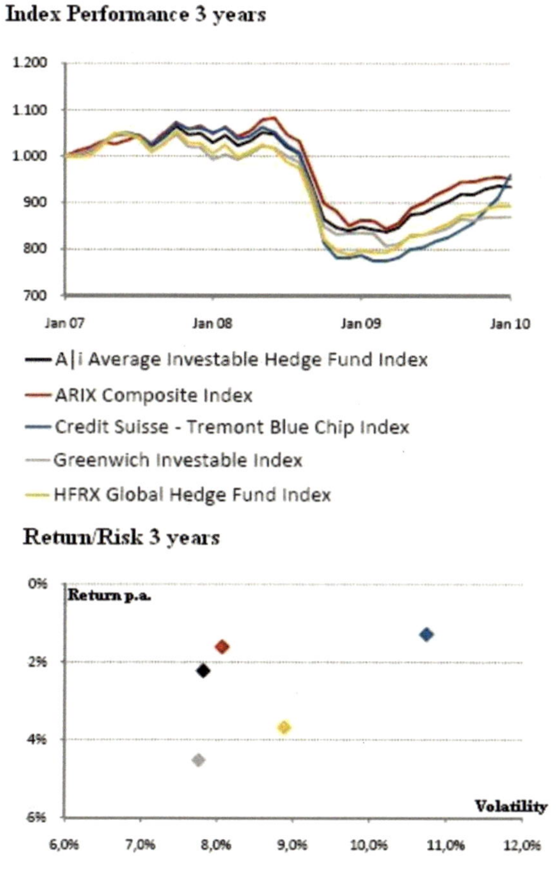
Index Performance 3 years
1.200
1.100
1.000
900
800
700
Jan 07
Jan 08
Jan 09
Jan 10
A|i Average Investable Hedge Fund Index
ARIX Composite Index
Credit Suisse - Tremont Blue Chip Index
Greenwich Investable Index
HFRX Global Hedge Fund Index
Return/Risk 3 years
Return p.a.
0%
2%
4%
6%
Volatility
6,0%
7,0%
8,0%
9,0%
10,0%
11,0%
12,0%

Figure 13

Target Market Size

There has been a clear trend in the global assets under management to deterioration in 2008. This is due to the world financial crisis and its recoverage in 2009.

38% of the global money is invested in equities. At the second place bonds cover 19% of global assets.

Figure 14

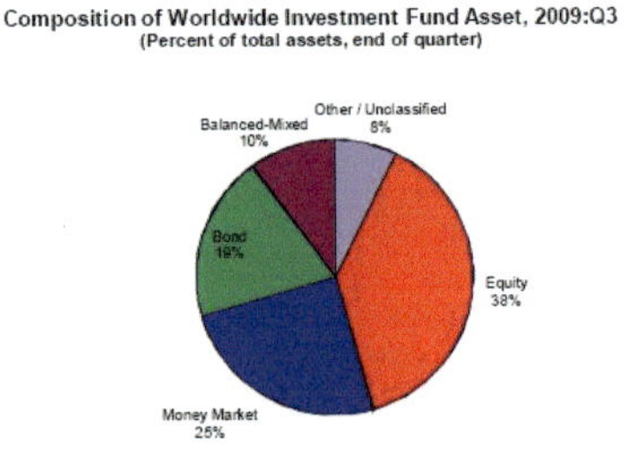

Figure 15

Largest hedge funds (January 2010)	**\$bn**
1. JP Morgan	50.4
2. Bridgewater Associates	43.6
3. Paulson & Co.	32.0
4. Brevan Howard Asset Management LLP	27.9
5. Soros Fund Management	27.0
6. D.E. Shaw Group	23.6
7. Och-Ziff Capital Management Group	23.5
8. Baupost Group	21.8
9. Man AHL	21.7
10. Angelo, Gordon & Co.	20.8

Table 6

Regulation under German Law (by EFAMA (2005))

Legal Form

Special funds are set up as German "Sondervermögen". This is a contractual type of fund. The fund's assets have to be kept strictly separate and are managed for investors' account. A Special fund may have only one institutional investor or many of them – the number is not limited. Relations between investors and the management company as well as the character of the fund are laid down in the contractual terms and conditions, which can be supplemented by side letters.

Manager, Custodian and Supervisory Authority

Special funds have to be managed by a "Kapitalanlagegesellschaft", that is a fund management company licensed under German law. For every Special fund there is a depositary bank, which can be either a German bank or a German branch of a foreign banking group."Kapitalanlagegesellschaften" are licensed and supervised by Bundesanstalt für Finanzdienstleistungsaufsicht (BaFin). In contrast, no authorization by BaFin is needed to set up a Special fund.

Reporting

According to the law, the management company has to present a short-form annual report for every Special fund at the end of each financial year. The report has to be audited and the auditor must summarise the results in a separate certificate. Practically, the annual report is of little importance to Special fund investors. They usually agree with the management company on an additional reporting that fits their individual needs with regard to form, content and frequency. No prospectus or other issuing document is required for Special funds.

Tax

For tax purposes an investment fund is a special purpose entity or a tax-free corporation. It is exempt from corporate income tax and trade tax. As a matter of principle, the fund does not pay tax on income from domestic and foreign stocks (dividends), domestic and foreign bonds (interest income), investment in money-market instruments or other short-term investments (interest income) which accrue to the fund gross without deductions.

Made in the USA
Monee, IL
12 September 2026

62973762R00036